Skyline 1

Workbook

Kate Fuscoe

MACMILLAN

Contents

Unit 1 Hello!

1 Meeting people

Language summary: asking and giving names

Use:
Use the verb *be* to ask for and give names.

Form:

What's (is)	your his her	name?
My His Her	name's (is)	John. / Mary.

1 Language work

a Put the conversation in the correct order.

.... Rome, Italy.

.... Teresa Agostini.

.... And where are you from?

..1.. What's your name, please?

.... Thank you.

b Circle the correct form.

1 What's *you* / *your* name?   My *name* / *name's* Paul.

2 Where *is* / *are* you from?   *I* / *I'm* from London.

3 What's *she's* / *her* name?   *She's* / *Her* name's Janet.

4 Where's *she* / *she's* from?   *She* / *She's* from Holland.

c First complete the questions. Then answer the questions for you.

1 What ...'s your name?   My ....

2 How do .... spell your name?   ....

3 Where .... you from?   ....

4 How .... you spell that?   ....

2 Word work: countries

Match the country with the capital city.

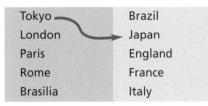

Tokyo — Brazil
London → Japan
Paris — England
Rome — France
Brasilia — Italy

3 Language work

a Match the object with the country. Then write a sentence.

sushi	France
roast beef	Japan
feijoada	Italy
pasta	England
champagne	Brazil

Sushi ‹is from Japan› ....

1 Feijoada ....

2 Pasta ....

3 Champagne ....

4 Roast beef ....

b Rewrite the sentences with contractions.

What is your name?   ‹What's your name?› ....

1 I am Susanne.   ....

2 Where is he from?   ....

3 He is from Uruguay.   ....

4 Where is she from?   ....

5 My name is Claudio.   ....

Language note

Normally people say:
She's from England.
not *She is* from England.

4 Skills work: reading and writing

a Look at the I.D. cards and answer the questions.

1   1 What's her last name?   ....

   2 What's her first name?   ....

   3 Where's she from?   ....

2   1 What's his last name?   ....

   2 What's his first name?   ....

   3 Where's he from?   ....

b Complete your own I.D. card.

1

IDENTITY CARD

Last name: Hatfield
First name: Jenny
International College
California, U.S.
STUDENT I.D. CARD

SIGNATURE   Jenny Hatfield

3

IDENTITY CARD

Last name:
First name:

SIGNATURE

2

IDENTITY CARD

Last name: Gonzalez
First name: Miguel
Excel Institute of English
Madrid, Spain
STUDENT I.D. CARD

SIGNATURE   Miguel Gonzalez

c Write questions for the I.D. card in exercise 4b.

1 What's ‹your last name› ....?

2 What's   ....?

3 Where   ....?

2 Introductions

Language note

Mr.	= man, married or single.
Mrs.	= married woman.
Miss	= woman, single or young.
Ms.	= woman, married or single.

In a store, hotel or restaurant:

sir = man. *ma'am* = woman.

1 Language work

Complete the conversations.

1 Bill: Jim, (1) ...This... is Heather.

   Jim: Nice to meet (2) .... Heather.

   Heather: Hello, Jim.

2 Sue: David, (3) .... Liz.

   David: Nice (4) ....

   Liz: (5) ....

3 Receptionist: Excuse me. Are (6) .... Maria Brown?

   Woman: Yes, I (7) ....

   Receptionist: You have a message, ma'am.

   Woman: Thank (8) ....

4 Waiter: (9) .... George Smith?

   Man: (10) .... am.

   Waiter: (11) .... , sir.

   Man: (12) ....

5 Joe: Good morning, Sue. How (13) .... you?

   Sue: I'm (14) .... , thanks. How about you?

   Joe: Fine.

6 Marta: (15) ....

   Jill: (16) ....

   Marta: (17) ....

2 Language work

> **Language note**
>
> For short affirmative answers, use the full form.
> *Are you Maria Brown?   Yes, I am.*
> For short negative answers, use the contraction.
> *Are you Maria Brown?   No, I'm not. / No, I am not.*

Circle the correct form. Then answer the questions for you.

Are *you* / *your* Ana? ....

1 Are *you* / *your* Venezuelan? ....

2 *Are* / *Is* your teacher English? ....

3 *Is* / *Are* it the morning now? ....

4 *Is* / *Are* you in class now? ....

3 Language work

a Match the sentences with the pictures.

1 ..E.. This is Rose.

2 .... Excuse me.

3 .... Nice to meet you.

4 .... My name's Martin.

5 .... Hi!

b Practice the expressions with a partner – or with yourself in the mirror!

3 Join the club

1 Word work: numbers

a Write the answers (as numbers).

1	2 x 3 =	..6..
2	1 + 8 =	....
3	13 - 2 =	....
4	20 ÷ 2 =	....
5	3 + 2 =	....
6	3 - 2 =	....
7	5 x 4 =	....
8	16 ÷ 2 =	....
9	20 - 3 =	....
10	12 + 7 =	....

b Write the numbers from exercise 1a as words in the word puzzle.

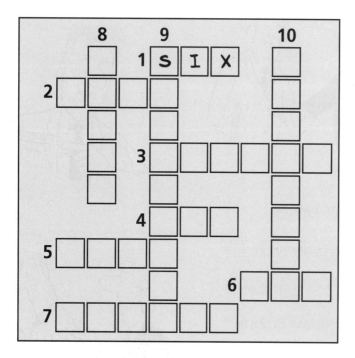

2 Language work

a Look at these telephone numbers. Say them.

044 3963 = oh four four, three nine six three.
3409 667 = three four oh nine, six six seven.

> **Language note**
> For telephone numbers, say *oh* for *0*. Say *three, three* for *33*.

b Now say these telephone numbers.

1 7825 449
2 625 4300
3 430 251
4 2788 002
5 881 7033

c First write some important telephone numbers here (include your own).
Then practice saying them.

> NAME   TELEPHONE NUMBER
> _____
> _____
> _____
> _____

3 Pronunciation work

a Put the words in the correct column, according to the stress.
All the words are from unit 1.

> **Language note**
>
> Words have syllables:
> *twen-ty* = 2 syllables
> *af-ter-noon* = 3 syllables
> Look at the stress in these words. Say them:
> *twen*ty   after*noon*

twenty	center	Internet	exercise	important	message	music
producer	commercial	morning	capital	alphabet		

Oo	oOo	Ooo
twenty	important	Internet

b Can you write more words in the table?

Unit 2 People and places

1 People at work

1 Language work

Language note
Remember to use *a* or *an* for singular jobs:
I'm teacher. ✘
*I'm **a** teacher.* ✔
*I'm **an** actor.* ✔

Look at the people in the pictures. Then complete the sentences about them.

I'm a ...... *taxi driver* ....

2 He's ....

4 She's ....

1 I'm an ....

3 He's ....

5 ....

2 Word work: occupations

a Find ten occupations in the word square.

B	A	N	K	E	R	F	E	R	O
D	R	E	I	C	J	U	D	O	P
O	C	P	A	I	N	T	E	R	T
R	H	O	G	M	V	I	S	D	I
P	I	L	O	T	W	S	I	E	C
A	T	I	A	N	L	T	G	N	I
L	E	H	T	I	C	M	N	T	A
A	C	T	O	R	K	Y	E	I	N
R	T	E	A	C	H	E	R	S	O
E	N	G	I	N	E	E	R	T	S

b Put the conversation in the correct order.

.... I'm a pilot.

..1... Hi, George.

.... Hi, Bill. This is my friend, Rita.
Rita's an engineer.

.... Nice to meet you too, Bill.
What do you do ?

.... Hi, Rita. Nice to meet you.

c Complete the occupations. Use your dictionary if you want.

He's a design.er.. .

1 He's a write....... .

2 She's a tennis play....... .

3 He's a politic....... .

4 She's a dance....... .

5 I'm a mathematic....... .

6 She's a sing....... .

7 I'm a music....... .

> **Language note**
>
> Notice how many occupations are made by adding
> *-or* , *-er* , or *-r* to a verb or noun:
> *an act**or**   a teach**er**   a drive**r***
> Words ending in *-ic* sometimes add *-ian* to make
> the occupation: *an electric**ian***

3 Pronunciation work

a Put the jobs in the correct column, according to the stress.

doctor   painter   reporter   journalist   inspector   musician
programmer   actor   architect

Oo	**oOo**	**Ooo**
doctor	reporter	journalist

b Can you write more words in the table?

2 New job

1 **Skills work:** reading and writing

a Read the information and write about the people.

STAR MEDIA INTERNATIONAL ⭐ STAR
Last name: JONES
First name: LUCY
Office: LONDON
Occupation: SECRETARY
SIGNATURE *Lucy Jones*

She's Lucy Jones.
She's a secretary.
She's from London.

STAR MEDIA INTERNATIONAL ⭐ STAR
Last name: WATANABE
First name: TAKASHI
Office: TOKYO
Occupation: DESIGNER
SIGNATURE *Takashi Watanabe*

2 ....
....
....

STAR MEDIA INTERNATIONAL ⭐ STAR
Last name: MULLER
First name: KATRIN
Office: BERLIN
Occupation: ACCOUNTANT
SIGNATURE *Katrin Muller*

STAR MEDIA INTERNATIONAL ⭐ STAR
Last name:
First name:
Office:
Occupation:
SIGNATURE

1 ....
....
....

3 I'm ....
....
....

b Complete your own I.D. card (3). Write about a new job for yourself.

2 **Word work:** countries and nationalities

Complete the list of countries and nationalities.

Japan – *Japanese*

1 Italy – ....

2 .... – Indian

3 Mexico – ....

4 .... – Turkish

5 Portugal – ....

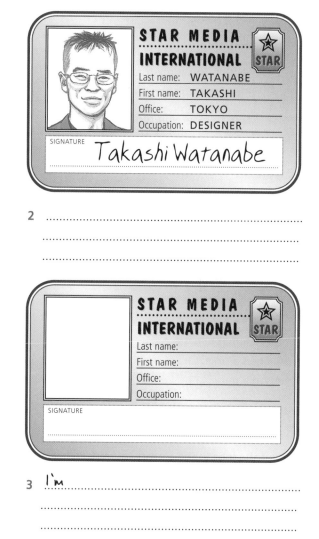

Language note

Many (but not all!) nationalities end in -ese, -ish, -an or -ian:

Japan**ese**   Span**ish**

Americ**an**   Austral**ian**

3 Pronunciation work

Put the nationalities in the correct column, according to the stress.

American	Canadian	English	Japanese	Colombian	Peruvian	Spanish
	German	Brazilian	Portuguese			

oOoo	Oo	ooO
American	English	Japanese

4 Language work

a Match the three columns in the table.

Subject	Verb	Contraction
I	are	I'm
You	are	We're
He / She / It	am	He's / She's / It's
We	are	You're
You	are	You're
They	is	They're

Language summary: verb *be*

Use:
Use the verb *be* to talk about your country of origin and your occupation.

Form:
I'm Australian.
You're a student.
She's Portuguese.
They're journalists.

b Circle the correct form. Then rewrite the sentences with contractions.

She (*is*) / *are* French. ....She's French.....

1 You *is* / *are* students. ....

2 They *is* / *are* Italian. ....

3 We *am* / *are* from Peru. ....

4 I *am* / *is* from Japan. ....

5 He *are* / *is* a teacher. ....

6 You *is* / *are* an engineer. ....

7 They *is* / *are* actors. ....

8 She *are* / *is* married. ....

9 You *are* / *is* Mexican. ....

10 He *is* / *are* Canadian. ....

3 On the Internet

1 Language work

a Put the words in the correct order to form questions.

what / name / your / is ?   *What is your name?*

1 from / where / you / are ?   .... ?

2 do / do / you / what ?   .... ?

3 you / are / student / a ?   .... ?

4 married / you / are?   .... ?

5 phone / number / is / your / what ?   .... ?

b Answer the questions in exercise 1a for you.

My name's ....   3 ....

1 ....   4 ....

2 ....   5 ....

c Circle the correct sentence.

(a) Are you a doctor?   b) Are you doctor?

1 a) Are she from Italy?   b) Is she from Italy?

2 a) Is he a architect?   b) Is he an architect?

3 a) You married?   b) Are you married?

4 a) Are you students?   b) Are you student?

5 a) Are they teachers?   b) They are teachers?

2 Word work: the Internet

Complete the information with the words in the box.

Australian	computer	name's	e-mail
Internet	user	from	student

My (1) *name's* Karen. I'm (2)........................ .

I'm (3)........................ Sydney. I'm a regular

Internet (4)........................ . I'm a (5)........................

and I use the (6)........................ to get information.

And I use (7)........................ to write to my friend,

Maria, in El Salvador. Maria isn't a student – she's

a (8)........................ programmer.

3 Skills work: reading

a Read the article and circle the correct answer for each space. Then check with your teacher (or an encyclopedia!).

1 a) 6000   (b) 600   c) 60

2 a) English   b) French   c) Spanish

3 a) 3   b) 4   c) 5

4 a) 150   b) 250   c) 350

5 a) 200   b) 300   c) 400

> **Glossary**
> *mother tongue:* your first language. If you are from Japan your mother tongue is probably Japanese.
> *second language:* not your first language, but a language you speak at work or school.
> *official language:* the official languages of Canada are English and French.
> *foreign language:* a language from another country.

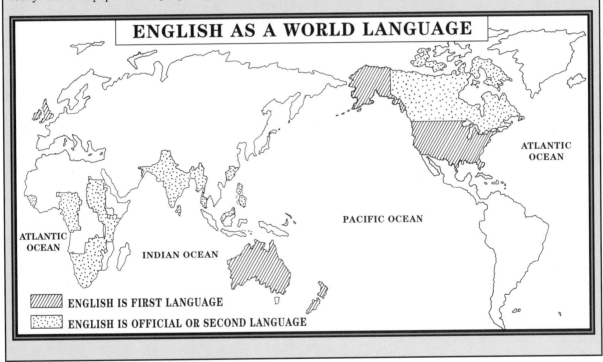

WORLD LANGUAGES

There are about (1) 600 languages in the world today. The most popular of these is (2) .... English is spoken on (3) .... continents, by more than a billion people. About (4) .... million people speak English as their mother tongue and more than (5) .... million use it as a second or official language. Children learn English at school as a foreign language. Adults learn at private schools, colleges and universities. It is the language of business, travel and politics.

ENGLISH AS A WORLD LANGUAGE

ATLANTIC OCEAN

ATLANTIC OCEAN

INDIAN OCEAN

PACIFIC OCEAN

▨ ENGLISH IS FIRST LANGUAGE

░ ENGLISH IS OFFICIAL OR SECOND LANGUAGE

b Complete the texts with the names of countries.

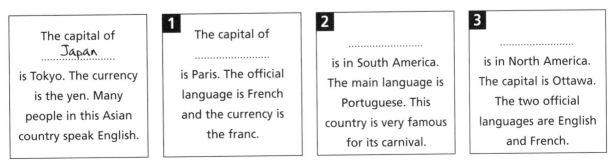

The capital of
Japan
is Tokyo. The currency is the yen. Many people in this Asian country speak English.

1 The capital of
....
is Paris. The official language is French and the currency is the franc.

2 ....
is in South America. The main language is Portuguese. This country is very famous for its carnival.

3 ....
is in North America. The capital is Ottawa. The two official languages are English and French.

Unit 3 Think green

1 An international conference

1 Word work: hotels

a Look at the words in the box. Are they usually facilities in a hotel or in a hotel room? Complete the spidergram with the words in the box.

> Internet access   gym   bath   sauna   TV   conference rooms   restaurant
> bar   telephone   mini-bar

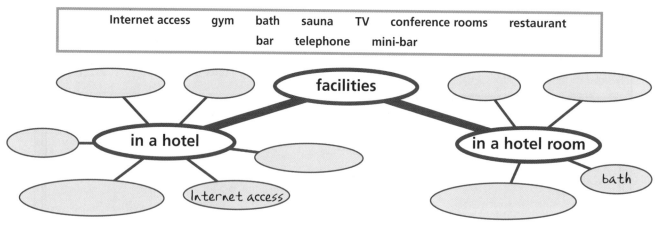

b Can you write some more words on the spidergram?

2 Skills work: reading

Choose the best hotel (A–D) for each traveler.

1 Names:
Peter and Marina Friedman
Occupations: dentist and architect
Ages: 36 and 34

In London: for a romantic weekend

3 Name:
George Spirino
Occupation: company director
Age: 48

In London: on business

2 Names:
Bob, Sue, Kerry and Tim Burrows
Occupations: engineer, teacher
and schoolchildren
Ages: 34, 33, 6 and 4
In London: for a weekend visit

4 Names:
Jill Wearing and Jan Fraser
Occupations: students
Ages: 19 and 21

In London: on vacation

.... A

Majestic Hotel *****

- *luxury hotel*
- *central location*
- *conference facilities*
- *free Internet access*

.... B

★★★★
H O T E L   P A R A D I S E

- restaurant
- sauna and swimming pool
- single or double rooms with bath

.... C

FLOWERS YOUTH HOSTEL

★ SINGLE ROOMS OR DORMITORY ★

★ BREAKFAST INCLUDED ★

★ FREE INTERNET ACCESS ★

.... D

GREEN'S HOTEL

– family rooms –

– TV in every room –

– breakfast included –

✵ ✵

3 **Word work:** numbers 1–100

Write the numbers as words.

	22	twenty-two	3	13	....	6	50	....
1	45	....	4	31	....	7	79	....
2	86	....	5	97	....	8	68	....

4 **Language work**

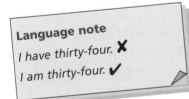

Language note
I have thirty-four. ✗
I am thirty-four. ✔

Language summary: talking about ages

Use:
Use the verb *be* to ask and say ages.

Form:

How old	are you?	I'm	seventeen.
	is he?	He's	
	is she?	She's	

Look at the pictures and decide how old the people are. Use *about* to show you are not sure.

1 He's about thirty.   2 ....   3 ....   4 ....   5 ....

2 The magnificent monarch

Language summary: present simple

Use:
Use the present simple to talk about routines or usual activities.
I / you / we / they **live** *in Rome.*

Form:
Use *do* to form questions, negatives and short answers.

Do you live in Rome?	Yes, I do.
	No, I don't.

1 Language work

a Circle the correct sentence.

a) Live you in Canada ? (b) Do you live in Canada ?

1 a) I no have a dog.   b) I don't have a dog.

2 a) Do you work in this office? Yes, I do.   b) Do you work in this office? Yes, I work.

3 a) We don't work in a hotel.   b) We not work in a hotel.

4 a) Like they to dance?   b) Do they like to dance?

b Answer the questions for you. Use short answers.

1 Do you live in a city? ....

2 Do you live in an apartment? ....

3 Do you have a computer? ....

4 Do you have a bicycle? ....

5 Do you play football? ....

6 Do you play golf? ....

> **Language note**
> Remember to use short answers.
> *Do you speak English?*
> *Yes, I do. / No, I don't.* ✔
> *Do you speak English?*
> *Yes, I speak.* ✘

c Make the sentences negative.

We speak Italian.   We don't speak Italian.

1 They like football. ....

2 I have a bicycle. ....

3 I like to dance. ....

4 You play tennis very well. ....

5 They live in Argentina. ....

2 Word work: mammals and insects

a Write the names of the insects and mammals.

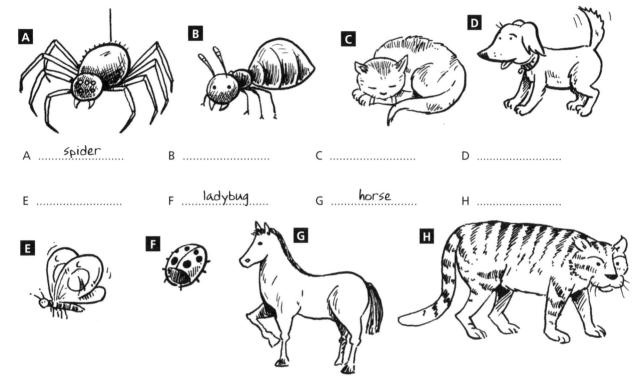

A ......spider......   B ....   C ....   D ....

E ....   F ......ladybug......   G ......horse......   H ....

b Look at exercise 2a. Which are insects and which are mammals? Put them in the correct column in the table.

Insects	Mammals
spider	

c Can you write some more insects and mammals in the table? Use your dictionary if you want.

d Answer the questions for you. Use short answers.

1 Do you like horses?   ....
2 Do you like cats?   ....
3 Do you like spiders?   ....
4 Do you like tigers?   ....
5 Do you like butterflies?   ....

e Look at the questions in exercise 2d and write two more questions with *like*. Then answer your questions.

1 .... ? ....
2 .... ? ....

3 An unusual job

Language summary: present simple (affirmative)

Use:
Use the present simple to talk about routines and regular activities.

Form:
For regular verbs the 3rd person affirmative (*he / she / it*) adds *-s* to the main verb. *Have*, *do* and *study* are irregular verbs.

I	live		lives
	eat	He	eats
You	work	She	work**s**
We	have	It	**has**
They	do		does
	study		stud**ies**

---

1 Language work

Circle the correct form in the sentences. Then mark the sentences T (true) or F (false).

Butterflies *lives /* (*live*) in Mexico.   T ✔   F ◯

1 I *have / has* toast for breakfast.   T ◯   F ◯

2 I *works / work* in the city.   T ◯   F ◯

3 My teacher *speak / speaks* Italian.   T ◯   F ◯

4 Tigers *lives / live* in Africa.   T ◯   F ◯

5 A bat *eats / eat* insects.   T ◯   F ◯

> **Language note**
> The verb *have* is irregular.
> *He* **has** *a dog.* ✔
> *He haves a dog.* ✗

Language summary: present simple (3rd person)

Use:
- Use *does* + subject + the main verb to make 3rd person questions.
- Use subject + *does not / doesn't* + the main verb to make 3rd person negative sentences.

Form:

Does	he your friend	live in Paris? study Portuguese?
She Peter	doesn't	work on weekends. speak Japanese.

2 Language work

First complete the questions with *does* or *do*.
Then write short answers.

......Do.... bats live in caves?   Yes, they do.................

1 .... you speak Italian ?   ....

2 .... your teacher speak Spanish?   ....

3 .... they speak English in the United States?   ....

4 .... we have English class on Tuesday?   ....

5 .... butterflies migrate?   ....

6 .... a spider eat insects?   ....

7 .... you like cats?   ....

> **Language note**
> Remember to use the infinitive for the main verb:
> Does he **have** a dog? ✔
> Does he **has** a dog? ✗

3 Skills work: reading

A STUDENT'S LIFE

Interviewer: What do you do, Suzi?

Suzi: I'm a student at U.C.L.A. I major in drama.

Interviewer: Do you like your classes?

Suzi: I love them! I want to be a famous actress one day.

Interviewer: What about your free time?

Suzi: I don't have much free time! I work in a bar on weekends. I also like to play tennis and dance.

Interviewer: Where do you live?

Suzi: I live in an apartment near the university, with two friends.

a Answer the questions about Suzi.

What does she do?   She studies drama..............

1 Does she like her classes?   ....

2 What does she do on weekends?   ....

3 Where does she live?   ....

4 Does she live alone?   ....

b Complete the questions for the answers about Ken.

What does Ken .....do....... ?   He's a teacher.

1 How old .... he?   Twenty-seven.

2 Where .... he live?   Los Angeles.

3 What .... he do on weekends?   He likes to go out with friends.

4 Does he .... with friends?   No, he doesn't. He lives alone.

5 Where does he .... ?   In a school in the city center.

Unit 4 Impressions

1 Famous faces

1 Word work: describing eyes and hair

a Look at the words in the box. Do they describe hair, eyes or both (hair and eyes)?
Complete the spidergram with the words in the box.

> brown   black   blond   red   gray   blue   green

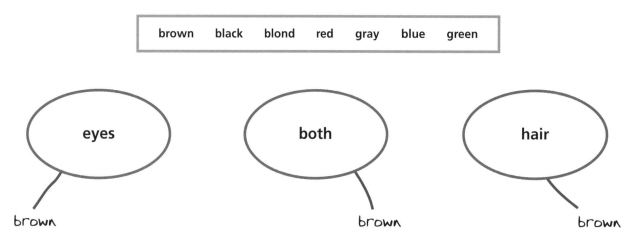

eyes
brown

both
brown

hair
brown

b Can you add more words to the spidergram?

2 Language work

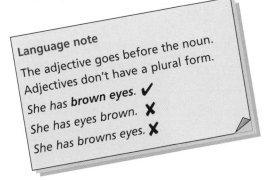

Language note
The adjective goes before the noun.
Adjectives don't have a plural form.
She has **brown eyes**. ✔
She has eyes brown. ✗
She has browns eyes. ✗

Language summary: descriptions

Use:
Use the verb *have* to talk about hair and eyes.

Form:			
subject +	***have*** +	**adjective** +	**noun**
She	has	brown	hair / eyes.

Use:
Use the verb *be* to talk about characteristics.

Form:		
subject +	***be*** +	**adjective**
He	is	tall / slim.

Circle the correct sentence.

a) She has hair brown.   (b) She has brown hair.

1a) She is red hair.   b) She has red hair.

2a) He has eyes of blue.   b) He has blue eyes.

3a) I have green eyes.   b) I have greens eyes.

4a) He has short.   b) He is short.

5a) I have dark hair.   b) I have hair dark.

3 Word work: descriptions

Find ten description words
(nouns and adjectives) in
the word square. They are
all in unit 4, lesson 1.

W	J	S	B	S	I	D	D	L	S
T	A	L	L	T	E	J	P	I	H
P	F	I	O	O	L	Y	T	F	O
O	O	M	N	B	G	P	U	A	R
W	O	E	D	H	K	F	E	L	T
E	Q	T	H	E	A	V	Y	P	O
I	I	H	A	I	R	U	E	A	H
G	O	O	N	G	E	A	S	H	X
H	P	I	L	H	B	L	A	C	K
T	U	H	B	T	D	A	B	E	T

4 Skills work: reading and writing

**a Read the description.
Is this Marco or Sven?**

> I am [very] tall.
> I have dark brown eyes.
> I have dark hair.
> My name's ....

b Write about the other person.

1 He's ....
2 He has ....
3 .... hair .
4 ....

c Write about yourself.

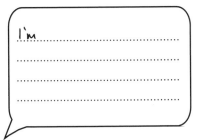
> I'm ....
> ....
> ....
> ....

OSCARS ACTING AGENCY

1. Marco Corleone
   Country: Italy
   Age: 27
   Height: 2m.
   Weight: 80 kilos
   Eyes: brown
   Hair: dark

OSCARS ACTING AGENCY

2. Sven Johansson
   Country: United States
   Age: 32
   Height: 1m.70
   Weight: 65 kilos
   Eyes: blue
   Hair: blond

2 Family connections

1 Word work: family

Complete the table with the words in the box.

| parent | woman | husband | son | aunt | cousin |
| father | brother | grandparent | baby | niece |

Male ♂	Female ♀
man	....
....	wife
....	daughter
uncle	....
nephew	....
....	mother
....	sister

Male or female 
parent
....
....
....
....

Language note

Plurals are usually formed by adding -s to the singular form.
one daughter – two daughters
Notice some irregular plurals:

Singular	Plural
man	men
woman	women
wife	wives
child	children
person	people

2 Language work

Language summary: possessive adjectives

Use:
Possessive adjectives go before nouns.

Form:

I You We They	eat	my your our their	lunch.
He She It	eats	his her its	

Language note

Remember that possessive adjectives do **not** have a plural form:
*They love **your** dogs.* ✔
They love yours dogs. ✗

a **Look at the photograph and complete the description with the words in the box.**

| daughter | sister | wife |
| brother | children | husband |

I'm Pat and this is my (1) ..husband... John.
These are our (2) .... , Joseph, Miles
and Rosie. Miles is married. His (3) .... 's
name is Jan. His (4) .... , Joseph, isn't
married. His (5) .... , Rosie, has a
boyfriend. Her boyfriend's name is Ricky.
We have one grandchild – Miles and Jan's
(6) .... Her name is Violet.
She's beautiful!

b **Look at your answers in exercise 2a. Then mark these sentences T (true) or F (false).**

John is Pat's husband.   T ✔   F ◯

1 Rosie is Pat's son.   T ◯   F ◯

2 Joseph and Miles are John's sons.   T ◯   F ◯

3 Violet is Pat's daughter.   T ◯   F ◯

4 Ricky is Jan's boyfriend.   T ◯   F ◯

5 Joseph is Violet's aunt.   T ◯   F ◯

Language note
Add -'s to a noun to show possession.
Her boyfriend's name is Ricky = The name
of her boyfriend is Ricky.

3 Skills work: reading and writing

a **Find four more mistakes in the text about Ben. Correct the mistakes.**

brother
This is my ~~sister~~, Ben. He is twenty-five.

He works in a bank. He's average height and slim.

His eyes are greens. He's married and your wife is

a teacher. Her name Maria.

They are two children – Joe and Sally.

Ben

b **Write about two members of your family (on a separate piece of paper).**

3 Dream date

1 Word work: sports and leisure activities

a Match the picture with the activity.

1 ....E.... cooking
2 .... swimming
3 .... dancing
4 .... reading
5 .... listening to music
6 .... running

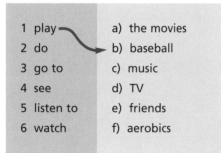

b Match the words to form names of activities.

1 play	a) the movies
2 do	b) baseball
3 go to	c) music
4 see	d) TV
5 listen to	e) friends
6 watch	f) aerobics

> **Language note**
> The verbs *like, love* and *hate* are followed by verb + *-ing* or a noun.
> *I like dancing.*
> *She doesn't like **sports**.*
> *We love going to the movies.*
> *He hates **pop music**.*

c Complete these sentences about you. Use the activities in exercise 1b.

1 I like ....

2 I hate ....

3 I don't like ....

4 I love ....

2 Skills work: reading and writing

a These students want to share a room.
Who are the best roommates?
Read the information and write the
names of roommates.

Language note
Your *major* is your principal subject at college.
*My **major** is biology.*
*I'm **majoring** in biology.*

1 ...... Julie ...... and ....
2 .... and ....

STUDENT PR

Name: Julie Lawson
Age: 24
Major: art history
Likes: art/museums/classical music
Dislikes: pop music/watching TV
Other information:
hates smoking!

STUDENT PR

Name: Jemima Johnson
Age: 21
Major: history
Likes: museums/music/going to movies
Dislikes: doing exercise/reading
Other information:
loves cooking for friends

STUDENT PR

Name: Jacky Brown
Age: 25
Major: sports therapy
Likes: tennis/aerobics/going to movies
Dislikes: watching TV/cooking
Other information:
allergic to cats

STUDENT PR

Name: Janice Jones
Age: 20
Major: psychotherapy
Likes: art/reading/cooking
Dislikes: pop music/sports
Other information:
has a cat

b Complete the two sentences explaining your answers in exercise 2a.

1 I put .... with .... because they both like ....
2 I put .... with .... because they both like ....

c Look at the people in exercise 2a. Who would you share a room with? Complete the sentence.

I would share a room with .... because we ....

Unit 5 House and home

1 Dormitory life

1 Word work:
things in a room

a Name the things in the pictures. Then write the names in the word puzzle. All the words are in unit 5, lesson 1.

b What is the word in the white boxes? ....

c Can you write the names of two more things in a bedroom or study?

1 ....

2 ....

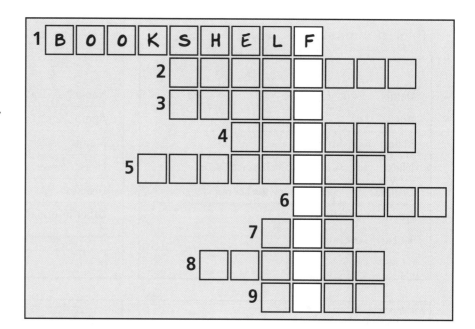

1 | B | O | O | K | S | H | E | L | F
2
3
4
5
6
7
8
9

2 Word work: colors

a Find ten colors in the word square.

D	F	Y	R	O	Y	A	K
P	U	R	P	L	E	H	W
R	A	E	S	K	L	O	H
T	G	D	Y	O	L	R	I
B	G	R	A	Y	O	A	T
L	U	B	R	O	W	N	E
U	I	L	Q	A	E	G	T
E	O	A	W	G	Y	E	G
A	L	C	G	R	E	E	N
E	R	K	B	P	O	U	R

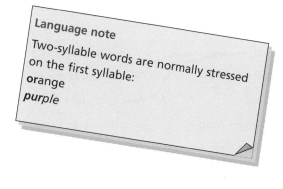

Language note
Two-syllable words are normally stressed on the first syllable:
orange
purple

b Look at the picture. What color are these things usually?

dog   <u>brown/black/white</u>   4 sky   ....

1 tree   ....   5 horse   ....

2 cloud   ....   6 grass   ....

3 sun   ....   7 sheep   ....

2 House plans

1 Word work: activities and rooms

Match the rooms with the activities you usually do there.

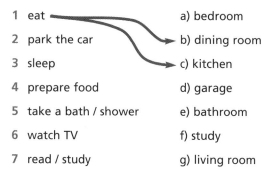

1 eat
2 park the car
3 sleep
4 prepare food
5 take a bath / shower
6 watch TV
7 read / study

a) bedroom
b) dining room
c) kitchen
d) garage
e) bathroom
f) study
g) living room

b Now write one sentence about what you do in each room in exercise 1a.

We eat in the dining room.

1 ....
2 ....
3 ....
4 ....
5 ....
6 ....

Language summary: *there is / are*

Use:
Use *there is / are* to talk about facilities.

Form:

Singular	Plural	
There's (is) a kitchen.	There are two bedrooms.	
There isn't (is not) a bathroom.	There aren't (are not) any chairs in the bedroom.	
Is there a garage?	Yes, there is. No, there isn't.	Are there any closets?	Yes, there are. No, there aren't.

---

2 Language work

a Look at the picture of a room on page 31. Then mark these sentences T (true) or F (false).

There are two sofas.   T ☑   F ◯

1 There are four chairs.   T ◯   F ◯
2 There isn't a stereo.   T ◯   F ◯
3 There's a TV.   T ◯   F ◯
4 There aren't any plants.   T ◯   F ◯
5 There's a rug.   T ◯   F ◯
6 There aren't any curtains.   T ◯   F ◯
7 There's a desk.   T ◯   F ◯

b Look again at the picture in exercise 2a. Answer the questions with short answers.

Are there any books?   *Yes, there are.*

1 Is there a computer?   ....

2 Is there a bed?   ....

3 Is there a TV?   ....

4 Are there any curtains?   ....

5 Is there a stereo?   ....

6 Are there any pens?   ....

7 Are there any plants?   ....

c **Circle the correct sentence.**

   a) There is a sofas.   (b) There is a sofa.

1 a) There aren't any books.   b) There are any books.

2 a) Is there a kitchen?   b) Is there any kitchen?

3 a) There are a closet.   b) There are three closets.

4 a) There isn't a car in the garage.   b) There aren't a car in the garage.

3 Word work: things in a room

Look at the words in the box. Which things are usually in which rooms?
Complete the word map with the words in the box.

bed   closet   rug   table   chair   refrigerator   stereo

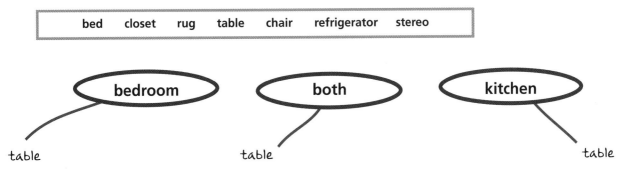

3 Lifestyles

1 Language work

Are these things countable or uncountable?
Write a / an or some.

........a.... cat
1 .... water
2 .... car
3 .... traffic
4 .... movie theater
5 .... apartment
6 .... furniture
7 .... pollution
8 .... neighbor

> **Language note**
> Use *a* or *an* for singular countable nouns.
> Use *some* for uncountable nouns and plurals.
> *I have a money.* ✘
> *I have **some** money.* ✔

Language summary: questions with *some / any*

Use:
• Use *any* or *some* for questions with uncountable and plural countable nouns.
• Use *any* when you don't know the answer to the question.
• Use *some* when you think you know the answer to the question.

Form:

Uncountable	Is there any **pollution**?	(You don't know.)
	Is there some **coffee**?	(You think the answer is *yes*.)
Plural countable	Are there any **cars**?	(You don't know.)
	Are there some **books** on the shelf?	(You think the answer is *yes*.)

2 Language work

Complete the sentences with *some* or *any*.

There isn't ...any.. traffic here on Sundays.

1 There is .... pollution in the river.
2 Are there .... movie theaters in your town? (Probably.)
3 Is there .... cold water in the refrigerator? (You don't know.)
4 There aren't .... parks near my house.
5 Are there .... Italian restaurants in the town? (You don't know.)
6 There are .... nice stores in the city.
7 Are there .... stores near here? (Probably.)
8 There's .... money in that bag.

> **Language note**
> Remember that we use *some* in affirmative sentences and *any* in negative sentences.
> *There are **some** plants in the living room.*
> *There aren't **any** plants in the living room.*

3 Skills work: reading and writing

a Puebla is a village in Spain. Predict the problems in Puebla before your read the article.

There are *some / aren't any* young people in Puebla.

1 There are *some / aren't any* animals.

2 There are *no / some* jobs.

3 There *is / isn't* a movie theater.

4 There are *some / no* bars.

5 There *is / isn't* a problem with water.

b Now read the article about Puebla and check your answers to exercise 3a.

> **Glossary**
>
> *population*: the number of people who live in a village / town / city
>
> *well*: a source of water (underground)
>
> *elderly*: old (for people)

PROBLEMS IN PUEBLA

Puebla is a small village in central Spain. The population of Puebla is currently twelve. Most of the twelve residents are over 70 years old. There are also two dogs and three cats!

There are no jobs here in the countryside for the young people of the village so they move to the cities. "We are too old to move" says Gracia Gomez (68), "but I would like to. It's really boring here!" In the evening there's nothing for people to do – no movie theater, no bar, no disco! But that's not really a problem for the elderly residents, who usually go to bed around 8 p.m. The other problem is that sometimes there isn't any water. The village depends on a number of wells and if it is a very hot summer, they have to buy water from the city and that is expensive.

68 year old Gracia Gomez

c Complete the postcard about the place where you live.
Choose from the words in the box (you do not need all of them).

Dear Barbara,

This is my (1) .... It is

very (2) .... There

(3) .... (4) ....

(5) .... I (6) ....

living here.

       Regards

       ....

> village   town   city
> big small interesting boring
> is   are
> a   some
> bar(s) movie theater(s) disco(s)
> like don't like

The World of Latin America Printed by ANOTHER PRINTERS LTD.

Unit 6 Work and leisure

1 Contrasts

1 Word work: sports and leisure activities

a Match the activities with the right equipment.

1 ....c.... baseball
2 .... tennis
3 .... aerobics
4 .... swimming
5 .... cooking
6 .... rollerblading

b Complete the sentences with *play*, *go* or *do*.

You ..play. tennis.

1 You .... dancing.
2 You .... aerobics.
3 You .... golf.
4 You .... judo.
5 You .... rollerblading.

> **Language note**
> Notice that we use different verbs for different sports.
> Use *play* when there is a ball: ***play*** *tennis*
> Use *go* when the activity ends in *-ing* : ***go*** *swimming*
> Use *do* for other activities: ***do*** *karate*

2 Pronunciation work

Put the jobs in the correct column, according to the stress.

| soccer   tennis   rock climbing   swimming |
| babysitting   basketball   baseball |
| weight training   cooking   rollerblading |
| reading   dancing   hang gliding |

Oo	Ooo	Oooo
soccer	rock-climbing	babysitting

3 Word work: days of the week

Put the letters in the correct order to form days of the week.

y d a n o m → M o n d a y

1 n u s a y d → ○○○○○○

2 d n s e y a d e w → ○○○○○○○○○

3 d t a u s e y → ○○○○○○○

4 a y f i r d → ○○○○○○

5 r u t a s y a d → ○○○○○○○○

6 t s u r h y a d → ○○○○○○○○

> **Language note**
> Days of the week
> begin with
> capital letters:
> on Tuesday ✔
> on tuesday ✗

4 Language work

First look at the table. Then write four sentences which are true for you. (You can use different activities.)

I usually	go (swimming) play (basketball) do (judo)	on	Monday. Friday. the weekend.

1 I ....

2 ....

3 ....

4 ....

2 Time rules, OK?

1 Language work

a Write the correct time for each clock. Choose from the times in the box. (You do not need all of them.)

| six ten | twelve o'clock | four fifteen | half past nine | one forty-five | ten to six |
| eight thirty | three thirty | ten after four | a quarter to one | | |

1 ...... *twelve o'clock* ......

3 ....

5 ....

2 ....

4 ....

6 ....

b Complete the conversations.

1 A: What ...... *time* ...... is it, please?
   B: It's ....
   A: Thank you.

2 A: What time .... , please?
   B: It's ....
   A: Thank you.

Language note

Use the verb *be* to ask and tell the time.
*What time **is** it?*
It's seven o'clock.
Remember that the verb is always singular.
It's three o'clock. ✔
They are three o'clock. ✗

36

3 A: .... , please?
   B: It's ....
   A: ....

4 A: ....
   B: ....
   A: ....

[12:50]

Language summary: frequency adverbs

Use:
Use frequency adverbs to talk about how often we do things.

0%   100%
───
    never   rarely   sometimes   often   usually   always

Language note
Frequency adverbs usually go before the verb, but they go after the verb *be*.

I never eat bananas. ✔   I am always happy. ✔

I eat never bananas. ✘   I always am happy. ✘

---

2 Language work

a Put the words in the correct order to form sentences.

never / I / cereal / for / eat / breakfast   I never eat cereal for breakfast.

1 often / on / tennis / Max / plays / Saturdays   ....

2 go / we / sometimes / swimming / weekends / on   ....

3 interesting / job / is / my / usually   ....

4 always / watches / she / TV / Friday nights / on ....

5 shopping / on / they / go / never / Mondays   ....

b Make true sentences using frequency adverbs.

Young people ......*often*...... go out on weekends.

1 Children .... watch TV in the evening.

2 College students .... work on weekends.

3 Babies .... go to a club or a bar.

4 My teacher .... speaks English to me.

5 My doctor .... speaks English to me.

c Rewrite the sentences with an appropriate frequency adverb.

I do my homework.   I always do my homework.

1 I study English on weekends.   ....

2 I speak English in my English class.   ....

3 I study grammar.   ....

4 I use a dictionary.   ....

5 I translate sentences into my language.   ....

6 I watch English language movies.   ....

3 Talent

> ## Language summary: talking about ability
>
> **Use:**
> Use *can* and *can't* to talk about ability.
> **Form:**
> *Can* and *can't* have the same form for **all** persons. Use a simple infinitive verb after *can* and *can't*.
>
> | I / You / He / She | can | play the violin. |
> |---|---|---|
> | We / You / They | can't (cannot) | dance the tango. |

1 Language work

a Complete the sentences with *can* or *can't*.

> **Language note**
> Remember:
> He **can** speak French. ✔
> He cans speak French. ✗

He ...can't... swim.

1 He .... cook.

2 She .... use a computer.

3 They .... ski.

4 He .... ice skate.

b Complete the sentences about yourself with *can* and *can't*.

1 I .... speak Spanish.

2 I .... swim.

3 I .... play golf.

4 I .... use a computer.

5 I .... play the piano.

6 I .... dance the tango.

> ## Language summary: asking about ability
>
> **Form:**
> The word order for questions with *can* is: *can* + simple infinitive verb.
>
> | Can | I / you / he / she
we / you / they | speak Japanese?
swim? |
> |---|---|---|

2 Language work

Answer the questions with short answers.

Can Brazilians speak Portuguese? _Yes, they can._

1 Can you use a computer? ....
2 Can your teacher dance the salsa? ....
3 Can bats swim? ....
4 Can you speak French? ....
5 Can a dog fly? ....

Language note
Remember:
Can he speak French? ✔
He can speak French? ✗
Do he can speak French? ✗

3 Skills work: reading and writing

a Read the information and choose the best job (A-C) for each person.

Glossary
position: a job
to work **full** *time*: to
work regular hours,
usually every day
part time: not full time
temporary: for a short
time, not permanent

A WANTED
Young babysitter, full of energy, to take care of two boys (3 years and 5 months) Mondays–Fridays.
Non-smoker essential. Ability to drive desirable.

B WANTED
Part time bar person for busy bar. Must work every weekend or 2 evenings a week.

C WANTED
Swimming pool attendant for summer vacation.
Ideal for students. Must be experienced swimmer with lifesaving certificate.
Temporary only.
Ability to drive desirable.

Name: Brendan Kent
Age: 22
Profile: Tourism Student
Abilities: Can speak French and Spanish. Can swim and drive.
NOTE: Vacation only

Name: Belinda Parks
Age: 22
Profile: Majored in sports
Abilities: Can speak German. Can swim and drive.
NOTE: Full time position preferred.

1 Job ....   2 Job ....

Name: Bill Hart
Age: 29
Profile: Politics student
Abilities: Can speak French. Can swim and drive.
NOTE: Smoker. No driver's license.

Name:
Age:
Profile:
Abilities:
NOTE:

3 Job ....   4 Your profile.

b Complete your own job profile. (4)

Unit 7 Travel

1 Vacations

1 Word work: vacations

a Complete the table with the words in the box.

| campsite with friends swimming sightseeing shopping |
| hotel dancing sunbathing beach taking photographs |
| playing tennis safari tour camping trip hostel |

Places to stay	Things to do	Types of holiday
with friends	swimming	beach

b Can you write more words in the table?

2 Word work: odd one out

Circle the word that is different from the others in each group.

	a) dance	b) ski	c) play tennis	d) watch TV
1	a) sunny	b) cloudy	c) temperature	d) rainy
2	a) spring	b) hot	c) summer	d) fall
3	a) Christmas	b) Easter	c) Independence Day	d) vacation
4	a) wife	b) grandson	c) daughter	d) sister
5	a) Monday	b) March	c) April	d) September
6	a) chair	b) table	c) cereal	d) bed
7	a) passionate	b) generous	c) leader	d) friendly

3 Skills work: reading and writing

a Read the information and choose the best holiday (A–C) for each person.

 A

THE RED SEA
● SCUBA DIVING ●
● WATER SKIING ● SWIMMING ●

All inclusive sports vacations in beautiful Israel. Singles or couples, fantastic international food and wine included.

B

MARVELLOUS MARRAKECH

Come to fabulous Morocco.
Visit the bazaars and
SHOP, SHOP, SHOP!
Eat and drink in the sun.
❋SPECIAL DISCOUNTS FOR STUDENTS❋

C

THAILAND
HISTORIC TOUR!

Come to Asia and enjoy the beauty of Thai culture.
Excellent Thai and international cuisine.
Tours to visit the historic capitals of Thailand - all with experienced tour guide and coach.
* Transportation to sites.

NAMES:
  Joan and Derek Peters
AGES:
  65 and 68
LIKES AND DISLIKES:
  both like exotic places and food.
N.B:
  Derek can't walk very far. Joan hates beaches.

Glossary
cuisine: the food of a country
bazaar: market or place for shopping, usually in Eastern countries
coach: a comfortable bus for long journeys

1 The best vacation for Joan and Derek is ....

NAMES:
  George Spiridon
AGE:
  32
LIKES AND DISLIKES:
  likes good wine and food, making new friends.
N.B:
  George has a desk job and likes to have a physical vacation.

NAMES:
  Anita Smith and Tina Gregson
AGES:
  25 and 26
LIKES AND DISLIKES:
  like making friends, food and shopping.
N.B:
  Anita and Tina are students.

3 The best vacation for Anita and Tina is ....

2 The best vacation for George is ....

b Which vacation in exercise 3a would you choose? Write about your choice.

I would prefer vacation .... because ....
....

2 Getting ready

1 Word work: clothes

a Write the names of the clothes in the word puzzle.

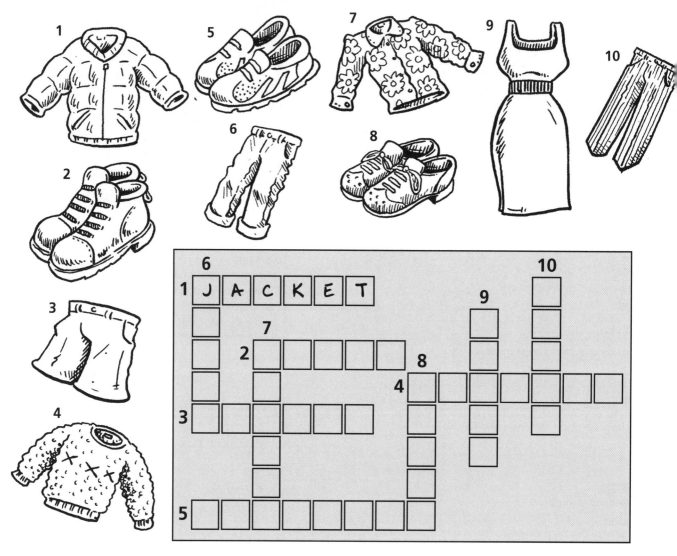

b Find two things in the puzzle that only women wear.

1 ....blouse........ 2 ....

c Find two things in the puzzle that you wear on your feet.

1 .... 2 ....

d Find two things in the puzzle that you don't wear to a formal party.

1 .... 2 ....

2 Language work

a Look at the picture and complete the sentences.

Jane is ....sunbathing........... .

1 Peter and Louise are ....

2 Gilly is ....

3 Sue ....

4 George and Joanna ....

5 Jack ....

Language summary: present progressive

Use:

Use this tense to talk about activity at this moment:
Can you be quiet! I'm watching TV.

Form:

I am (I'm)	swimming.
You are (You're)	
He / She / It is (He's)	reading.
We are (We're)	
They are (They're)	skiing.

b Answer the questions about the picture in exercise 2a. Use a short answer.

Is Jack taking a photograph?   Yes, he is.

1 Is Jane reading?   ....

2 Are Peter and Louise swimming?   ....

3 Is Sue sunbathing?   ....

4 Are George and Joanna playing tennis?   ....

5 Is Gilly eating?   ....

Language summary: present progressive

Form:

Questions: *be* + subject + verb + *ing*

Are you	sunbathing?	Yes, I am.
		No, I'm not.
Is he	swimming?	Yes, he is.
		No, he isn't.
		No, he's not.
Are they	reading?	Yes, they are.
		No, they aren't.
		No, they're not.

c Circle the correct sentence.

a) I am wearing a swimsuit.   b) I wearing a swimsuit.

1 a) I'm not eating steak.   b) I amn't eating steak.

2 a) Do you are staying in Italy?   b) Are you staying in Italy?

3 a) Are your sister working in a bank?   b) Is your sister working in a bank?

4 a) They are living in Colombia?   b) Are they living in Colombia?

43

3 Final destination

Language summary: present simple / present progressive
Use:
- Use the present simple to talk about regular activities.
  *He **plays** golf **on the weekends**.*
- Use the present progressive to talk about current or temporary activities.
  *He's **talking** to someone on the phone **at the moment**.*
  ***I'm staying** with a friend **for a week**.*

Language note
Don't use adverbs of frequency with the present progressive:
I usually eat toast for breakfast. ✔
I am usually eating toast. ✗

1 Language work

a Circle the correct answer.

Do you smoke?
  a) Yes, I am.   b) Yes, I do.   c) Yes, I smoke now.

1 Where do you work?
  a) I am working at the moment.   b) I work in a bank.   c) Yes, I do.

2 Where are you staying in London?
  a) No, I'm not.   b) I'm staying with my sister.   c) I stay in a hotel.

3 What are you wearing today?
  a) Yes, I am.   b) I usually wear jeans.   c) I'm wearing a dress.

4 Do you like New York?
  a) Yes, I like.   b) Yes, I am.   c) Yes, I do.

b Form the questions.

1 What / you / wear / now?   *What are you wearing now?*
2 What / you / usually / wear?   .... ?
3 What / you / usually / eat for breakfast?   .... ?
4 What / you / usually / do on weekends?   .... ?
5 What / you / study / now?   .... ?
6 What / you / usually / study?   .... ?

c Answer the questions in exercise 1b about yourself.

1 I'm ....
2 ....
3 ....
4 ....
5 ....
6 ....

2 Word work: collocation

a Match the verb with the appropriate noun to make a phrase.

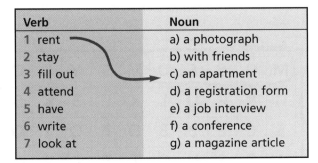

Verb	Noun
1 rent	a) a photograph
2 stay	b) with friends
3 fill out	c) an apartment
4 attend	d) a registration form
5 have	e) a job interview
6 write	f) a conference
7 look at	g) a magazine article

b Complete the sentences. Choose from the phrases in exercise 2a.

A journalist usually ...*writes magazine articles*... .

1 You usually .... when you stay in a hotel.

2 Doctors .... in different countries all over the world

3 Most people like to .... after their vacation.

4 Your vacation can be cheaper if you .... and not in a hotel.

5 It's expensive to .... or a house in the city center.

6 You usually .... before a company offers you a position.

3 Language work

Complete the conversation with the words in the box.

do	are	about	staying
doing	I'm	love	studying

A: This is a nice place.

B: Yes. Where (1) .....*are*..... you from?

A: (2) .... from Australia.

   How (3) .... you?

B: I'm from Germany.

A: What are you (4) .... in Boston?

B: I'm (5) .... English.

A: Where are you (6) .... ?

B: With an American family.

A: That's interesting.

   (7) .... you like it here?

B: Yes, I (8) .... it!

Unit 8 Around town

1 Places of interest

1 Word work: places in a city

a Find ten places in a city in the word square.

M	U	S	E	U	M	S	Y	U	O
U	P	R	U	L	K	U	S	K	B
S	C	E	B	B	O	P	Q	T	O
I	E	S	H	O	T	E	L	I	O
C	Z	T	X	C	G	R	U	D	K
S	C	A	F	E	O	M	J	I	S
T	L	U	H	F	D	A	W	S	T
O	A	R	L	P	A	R	K	C	O
R	A	A	B	A	N	K	M	O	R
E	U	N	E	R	T	E	T	Y	E
A	W	T	E	U	F	T	H	K	M

b Where am I? Write the names of the places. They are all in the word square.

You look at very old objects here. ......*a museum*......

1 You buy food here. ....

2 You go for a walk here. ....

3 You have dinner here. ....

4 You buy CDs and cassettes here. ....

5 You keep money here. ....

6 You go dancing here. ....

7 You can stay here. ....

c Write definitions for two more places from the word square.

1 *You* .... 2 ....

2 Language work

a **Look at the map and mark the sentences T (true) or F (false).**

The bank is across from the auditorium.   T ✓   F ◯

1 The restaurant is next to the hotel.   T ◯   F ◯

2 There's a supermarket on the corner of Lincoln Avenue and Main Street.   T ◯   F ◯

3 There's a cafe near the bank.   T ◯   F ◯

4 There's a movie theater on Jefferson Street.   T ◯   F ◯

5 The park is near the museum.   T ◯   F ◯

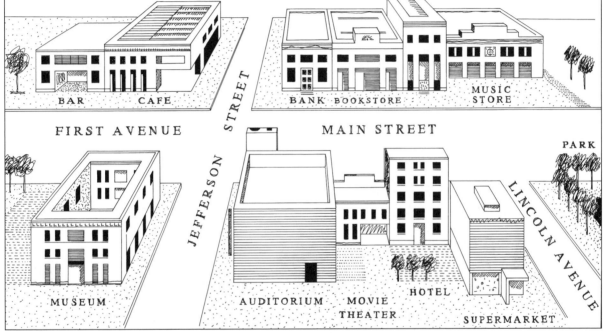

b **Look at the map in exercise 2a. Complete the sentences with *of*, *on*, *to*, or *from*.**

There's a bank ....on........ the corner ....of........ Main Street.

1 The supermarket is next .... the hotel.

2 There's a museum across .... the cafe.

3 There's a bar .... First Avenue.

4 The auditorium is .... the corner .... Jefferson Street and Main Street.

5 There's a restaurant next .... the music store.

c **Write about the facilities in a town you know.**

There's a ....

....

....

2 Plans for the weekend

1 Word work: entertainment

a Look at the words in the box. Do they describe a type of movie or a type of music?
Complete the spidergram with the words in the box.

action   rock   classical   classic   comedy   jazz   science fiction   drama   pop   opera

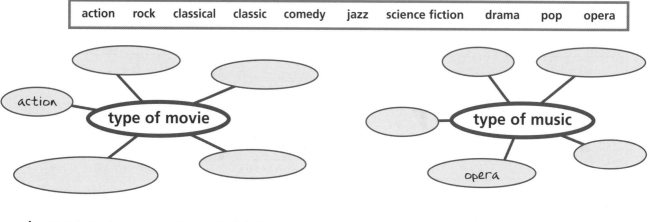

action

type of movie

type of music

opera

b Match the famous people and their jobs.

pop singer   actress   rock group   classical musician   actor

Vanessa Mae

Johnny Depp

Celine Dion

Oasis

Sandra Bullock

Sandra Bullock   1 Celine Dion   2 Vanessa Mae   3 Oasis   4 Johnny Depp

is _an actress_ .   is ....   is ....   is ....   is ....

c Complete the sentences with your own opinions.

1 I like .... music.   4 I like .... movies.

2 I don't really like .... music.   5 My favorite actor is ....

3 My favorite singer is ....   6 My favorite movie is ....

2 Skills work: reading and writing

Read the movie review of *French Kiss*.
Then write a similar review
about a movie you know.

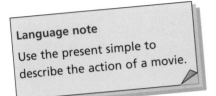

Language note
Use the present simple to
describe the action of a movie.

MOVIE REVIEW

FRENCH KISS is a romantic comedy
starring Meg Ryan and Kevin Kline.
She is an American in Paris and he is
a French criminal. They have a lot of
adventures and fall in love by
accident!

.... is a(n) .... movie starring ....

....

3 Language work

a Complete the table
with the phrases in the box.

go swimming	Let's …
Fine	tonight
Do you want to …	go for a drink
Good idea!	have dinner
on Wednesday	tomorrow
OK.	go to a movie

Making Suggestions	Social activity	Time phrase	Agreeing
	go swimming		

b Put the conversation in the correct order.

.... Fine. Let's meet at the restaurant
at nine o'clock.

.... OK. See you there!

...1... Do you want to have dinner tonight?

.... I prefer French I think. How about
Le Gavroche?

.... Good idea. Let's go to the new Italian
place near my house.

3 Honeymoon

1 Language work

a Put the words in the correct order to form sentences.

what / doing / Tuesday / are / you / on?   What are you doing on Tuesday? ....

1 going / with / to / movies / the / Jamie / I'm.   ....

2 driving / we're / beach / the / to / weekend / this.   ....

3 studying / with / all / day / Janice / I'm.   ....

4 working / Saturday / on / he's.   ....

5 wedding / you / Martin's / going / are / to ?   ....

b Look at Jennifer's date book. Then answer the questions about her plans.

Is Jennifer working on Monday?

Yes, she is. ....

1 Is Jennifer going out on Tuesday?

....

2 What's she doing on Wednesday?

....

3 Is she going out on Thursday?

....

4 What's she doing on Friday?

....

5 What's she doing on Saturday?

....

9 MONDAY

   teach all day

10 TUESDAY

   movie with Karen

11 WEDNESDAY

   yoga (with Kirsty)

12 THURSDAY

13 FRIDAY

   DINNER WITH JOSEPH!!!

14 SATURDAY

   Shopping and movie

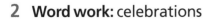

2 **Word work:** celebrations

Complete the definitions with the special days in the box.

| wedding day   Christmas Day   birthday |
| wedding anniversary   Independence Day |

> **Language note**
>
> Remember to use capital letters for public holidays, but not for personal ones:
>
> **C**hristmas **D**ay
>
> *M*y **b**irthday
>
> An *anniversary* is the celebration of an event each year – usually marriage.
>
> Your *birthday* is **not** an anniversary.

December 25 is ...Christmas Day...... .

1 It's their .... tomorrow, and then they are going on their honeymoon.

2 July 4 is .... in the United States.

3 Johnny is eight years old today – it's his ....

4 10 years of marriage – today is our tenth ....

3 **Skills work:** reading and writing

a Read about three celebrations. Write the names of the special days in the spaces. (Choose from the special days in exercise 2a.)

C

I'm really excited about .... We're going out for dinner in a restaurant this year – with lots of friends. We're having drinks in a local bar first, then there are fireworks in the town square and live music. It's going to be excellent!

A

I'm really excited about our .... .We're going out for dinner in a restaurant. Just the two of us and no children, which is very unusual! I can't believe we've been together for twenty years.

I'm really excited about my .... We're all going out for dinner in a pizza restaurant – about twenty of us! They're providing a cake too. After dinner we're going dancing at a club.

B

Glossary
Fireworks are used in many celebrations

b Write about a celebration you are planning. (You can invent one if you want!)

I'm really excited about ....

....

Unit 9 Bon appétit!

1 Good food

1 Word work: food

a Find ten foods in the word square. Use the pictures to help you.

A	P	P	L	E	Q	L	O
V	E	R	H	M	G	E	L
O	Y	O	G	U	R	T	M
C	O	R	N	O	I	T	G
A	E	M	W	R	C	U	S
D	R	Y	O	B	E	C	Z
O	C	F	I	S	H	E	F
N	Z	R	L	R	E	T	O
M	I	L	K	E	E	G	G
P	X	Q	M	T	Y	I	I

b Complete the table with the words in the box.

apples   beans   milk   oranges   strawberries   bananas   cheese
yogurt   butter   lettuce   peas   potatoes

Fruit	Dairy	Vegetables
apple		

c Can you write more words in the table?

Language summary: countable and uncountable nouns

Use:
• You **can** use numbers with countable nouns.
• You **cannot** use numbers with uncountable nouns.

Form:
Countable nouns have a singular and plural form.
Uncountable nouns do not have a plural form.

Countable	Uncountable
I like bananas.	I like cheese.
There **are** two bananas.	There **is** some cheese.

Language note
Liquids are usually uncountable:
There is some **milk** in the refrigerator.

2 Language work

a Decide if the foods in the list are countable or uncountable. Write C (countable) or U (uncountable).

..C.. strawberry   3 .... sugar   7 .... oil

..U.. milk   4 .... rice   8 .... potato

1 .... orange   5 .... pork   9 .... beef

2 .... yogurt   6 .... egg   10 .... avocado

b What food do you like? Complete the sentences with countable or uncountable nouns.

Oranges.... are nice.

1 .... is delicious.

2 .... are delicious.

3 I love ....

4 I hate ....

5 My favorite food is ....

6 My favorite international food is ....

7 .... aren't very good.

3 Skills work: writing

Make the text true for your country. Choose words from the list and write them in the spaces.

In my country, people (1) .... a lot of meat. We (2) .... a lot of salads. The main carbohydrate is (3) .... Our food is (4) .... Our main meal is (5) .... We usually eat (6) .... We (7) .... have (8) .... with a meal. We (9) .... have a dessert such as ice cream or fruit.

1 a) eat   b) don't eat   c) sometimes eat
2 a) eat   b) don't eat   c) sometimes eat
3 a) rice or pasta   b) potatoes   c) bread
4 a) not spicy   b) spicy   c) varied
5 a) in the afternoon b) in the evening   c) in the morning
6 a) around the table b) in front of the TV c) in the garden
7 a) sometimes   b) never   c) usually
8 a) wine   b) water   c) cola
9 a) don't usually   b) usually   c) always

2 Hungry?

1 Word work: meals

a Decide when you usually have these foods and drinks – for breakfast, lunch or dinner?
Complete the table with the words in the box. (Some words may go in more than one column.)

| coffee | salad | toast | cereal | yogurt | wine | a sandwich | orange juice | roast beef |

Breakfast	Lunch	Dinner
coffee		

b Can you write more words in the table?

c Complete the sentences about yourself.

1 I usually eat .... for breakfast.
2 My main meal of the day is ....
3 I eat dinner at about ....
4 I drink coffee ....

Language summary: *would like*

Use:
Use *would like* to express *want* in a polite way.
Form:
The form is the same for all persons.

I		
You	would like	a drink.
She	('d like)	something to eat.
They		

Language note

Notice the usual response forms to an offer made with *would you like*:
Would you like a cup of tea?
Yes, please. ✔
No, thanks. ✔
Yes, I would like. ✘

54

2 Language work

Circle the correct sentence.

a) What you like to drink?   (b) What would you like to drink?

1 a) I like some yogurt, please.   b) I'd like some yogurt, please.

2 a) I'd like some roast beefs.   b) I'd like some roast beef.

3 a) I'd like some cheese, please.   b) I'd like a cheese, please.

4 a) Would you like to order now?   b) Do you like to order now?

3 Language work

a Decide if the sentences are spoken by a guest or a waiter.

1 .....Guest..... Can I have a table by the window?

2 .... Would you like any vegetables with that?

3 .... Yes, of course. Would you like to sit here?

4 .... Mineral water, please.

5 .... Yes, I'd like grilled chicken, please.

6 .... Are you ready to order?

7 .... And what would you like to drink?

8 .... I'd just like a salad, please.

b Put the sentences in exercise 3a in the correct order to make a conversation.

1, 3 ....

c Circle the most appropriate response to the questions.

Would you like salad with that?

a) Yes, I am.   (b) No, thank you.   c) I like vegetables.

1 Are you ready to order?

a) How much is it?   b) Yes, I do.   c) Yes, I am.

2 What would you like to drink?

a) I like water.   b) Water, please.   c) I want water.

3 Would you like some coffee?

a) Yes, please.   b) Yes, I like.   c) No, I don't like.

4 Do you like beef?

a) Yes, I would.   b) Yes, I do.   c) Yes, I like.

3 What's cooking?

1 Word work: cooking

a Match the verbs with the pictures.

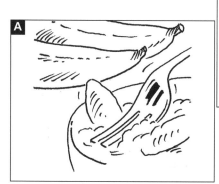

1 add / put ...F..
2 stir ......
3 mash ......
4 chop ......
5 serve ......
6 mix ......

b Complete the sentences with the words in the box.

| mash | stir | add | chop | mix | serve |

You can ....*serve*.... this dish hot or cold.

1 You .... avocados to make guacamole.

2 You .... soup while you are cooking it.

3 You .... salt and pepper to food at the table.

4 You .... an onion before cooking it.

5 You .... eggs to make an omelet.

Language summary: imperatives
Use:
Use the imperative form of the verb to give instructions, for example, in a recipe.
Form:
The affirmative form: infinitive without *to*.
Take two eggs.
Add salt and pepper.
Chop the vegetables.

Language note
Notice the prepositions used with these verbs:
You **add** sugar **to** your coffee.
You **put** sugar **in** your coffee.

2 Language work

a Match the beginnings and ends of the sentences.

1 Chop   a) with bread.

2 Add   b) the onions.

3 Blend   c) the tomatoes and add them to the pan.

4 Stir   d) cream or milk into the soup.

5 Fry   e) the onions in some oil or butter.

6 Serve   f) salt and pepper to taste.

b Write the instructions from exercise 2a in the correct order to complete the recipe for tomato soup.

T O M A T O S O U P

INGREDIENTS: METHOD:

1 small onion   First *chop the onions* ....

100g butter / oil   Then fry ....

1 can tomatoes   After that ....

half a cup milk/cream   ....

salt and pepper   Next ....

                      Add ....

                      Finally ....

3 Skills work: writing

Make a recipe card for a simple recipe. Write the ingredients and the instructions.

....

INGREDIENTS: METHOD:

....   First ....

....

....

....

....

....   Finally ....

Unit 10 Life stories

1 Personal history

Language summary: past simple (affirmative)

Use:

Use the past simple to talk about completed past events.

Form:

• For regular verbs add -ed to the verb: *want – want**ed***

• If the verb ends in e add -d: *move – mov**ed***

• If the verb ends in *y*, change to -*ied*: *marry – marr**ied***

• Irregular verbs are all different and you have to learn them! See the list of irregular verbs at the back of the Student's Book.

• The form is the same for all persons.

I	walk**ed** across the street.
She	lik**ed** the movie.
They	fr**ied** eggs for breakfast.

---

1 Language work

a Find the past simple form of these verbs in the word square.

> go   be (x 2)   act   become   have   grow up
>
> marry   get   want   move

M	A	R	R	I	E	D	G
A	C	M	O	V	E	D	O
S	T	C	H	N	W	O	T
B	E	C	A	M	E	W	A
R	D	L	D	E	R	E	W
A	F	H	D	L	E	N	A
G	R	E	W	U	P	T	S
W	A	N	T	E	D	C	S

b Complete the table with the past
simple verb forms from the word
square in exercise 1a.

Regular	Irregular
acted	

c Complete the sentences with past simple
verb forms from the table in exercise 1b.

Marilyn Monroe ....acted.......... in the movie *Some Like it Hot.*

1 John Lennon .... Yoko Ono in 1969.

2 Gloria Estefan .... born in Havana.

3 Eva Peron .... the wife of the president of Argentina in 1961.

4 The singer, Madonna, ... two children – Lourdes and Rocco – in the 1990s.

5 Keanu Reeves .... in Canada, but he wasn't born there.

2 Word work: personal history

**Complete Maria Pereira's personal history with the past simple of the verbs in the box.
(You do not need to use all the verbs.)**

go to school
marry
graduate
be born
get a divorce
have a child / children
grow up
move
start work
be
study

I (1) ....was born.......... in 1963, in a small village in the north of Brazil.

When I (2) .... ten we (3) .... to Rio de Janeiro and I

(4) .... there. I (5) .... from high school in 1980 and

(6) .... in an architect's office. Two years later I (7) .... an architect.

After some time we (8) .... – our first in 1988 and then another in 1994. They are

growing up very fast!

2 Life changes

> ### Language summary: past simple (negative)
> **Form:**
> For regular and irregular verbs use *didn't* (*did not*) + main verb.
> The form is the same for **all** persons. The verb *be* is different.
>
> | I
He
We
They | didn't
(did not) | like the movie.
go there. |
> | --- | --- | --- |
> | I
He | wasn't
(was not) | happy.
hungry. |
> | We
They | weren't
(were not) | |

1 Language work

a Circle the correct sentence.

    a) He didn't liked her hat.   (b) He didn't like her hat.

1 a) She didn't go to the party.   b) She didn't went to the party.

2 a) They hadn't a car at that time.   b) They didn't have a car at that time.

3 a) You wasn't at school yesterday.   b) You weren't at school yesterday.

4 a) They didn't move to New York.   b) They didn't moved to New York.

5 a) We didn't be on vacation in July.   b) We weren't on vacation in July.

b Make the sentences negative.

They liked fish.   They didn't like fish.

1 We went to the park.   ....

2 He was a good teacher.   ....

3 She studied math and chemistry.   ....

4 They were at home yesterday.   ....

5 He had a girlfriend last year.   ....

c Write three true sentences about last weekend. Use the words in the box.

study English   go to a bar   play tennis   watch TV   eat fish   read a newspaper   work

1 ....

2 I didn't ....

3 ....

2 Skills work: reading

a Before you read the article, answer these questions.

1 Can you name three kinds of meat?

....

2 Can you name three alternatives to meat?

....

3 What is the difference between a *vegan* and a *vegetarian*?

....

b Read the article about Heather George. Then mark the sentences T (true) or F (false).

HEATHER GEORGE *"I often just ate the vegetables"*

When I was a child, I didn't like meat very much and became a vegetarian when I was about twelve. It was a problem for my mom because there weren't as many vegetarian products as there are today. She was very inventive but I often just ate the vegetables from the family meal while everyone had roast beef! I became a vegan – stopped eating dairy products – when I was a college student because I learned about factory farming methods. I started drinking soya milk and eating new soy-based foods like *tofu*. When I got married, my husband John was a meat-eater, but he soon converted! Now my children are growing up vegetarian, but if they want to eat meat when they are older, they can.

Glossary
vegetarian: someone who doesn't eat meat
vegan: someone who doesn't eat meat or animal products, such as butter
factory farming: very intensive farming

Heather became a vegetarian because she didn't like meat. T ✔ F ○

1 When Heather was ten years old, she was a vegetarian. T ○ F ○

2 Heather stopped eating meat when she was in college. T ○ F ○

3 Heather eats eggs and cheese now. T ○ F ○

4 Heather's husband ate meat before they married. T ○ F ○

5 Heather's children eat meat. T ○ F ○

3 Romance and tragedy

Language summary: past simple (*wh-* questions)

Form:

• For regular and irregular verbs use:

wh- questions + did + subject + main verb.

• The form is the same for **all** persons.

Where	did	you go?
When		she start work?
What	did	they say?

• The verb *be* is different. Use *wh-* question + *be* + subject.

Where	was	she?
Who	were	the children?

1 Language work

a Complete the questions in this interview.

A: Where (1) .... *did you go* .... last weekend?

B: I went to a party

A: Where (2) .... the party?

B: At Giorgio's house.

A: What (3) .... drink?

B: I drank wine.

A: Who (4) .... meet there?

B: I met Giuliana.

A: When (5)................................. home?

B: I got home around 3:00 a.m!

b Put the words in the correct order to form questions.

yesterday / do / what / you / did?   *What did you do yesterday?*

1 go / Gillian / weekend / the / on / where / did? .... ?

2 party / was / when / the? .... ?

3 names / were / their / what? .... ?

4 Ann / school / to / get / did / how? .... ?

5 Shakespeare / did / when / die? .... ?

2 Word work: relationships

Match the verbs with the pictures.

1 ...D.. you marry

2 .... you meet someone

3 .... you go to a party

4 .... you go on your honeymoon

5 .... you fall in love

6 .... you go out together

3 Language work

a **Complete the text about Sally and Harry with the verbs in exercise 2a.**

This is my husband Harry. In 1994 I (1) ......went...... to a party and I (2) .... Harry. We (3) .... together for about two years and (4) .... in love slowly. Harry asked me to marry him when we were on vacation in Greece in August 1995. We (5) .... a year later in a little church in my village. There were about 200 guests. We (6) .... to Italy on our honeymoon. It was wonderful!

b **Form questions about Sally and Harry.**

Where / meet?   Where did they meet?..............................

1 When / go / Greece?   .... ?

2 When / marry?   .... ?

3 Where / marry?   .... ?

4 Where / go / honeymoon? .... ?

Unit 11 Looking back

1 A busy week

1 Word work: collocations

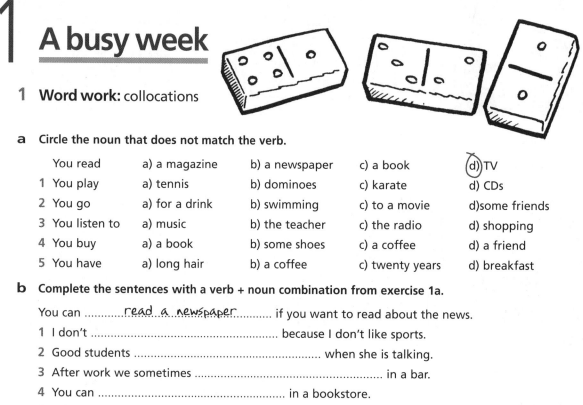

a Circle the noun that does not match the verb.

	You read	a) a magazine	b) a newspaper	c) a book	**d) TV**
1	You play	a) tennis	b) dominoes	c) karate	d) CDs
2	You go	a) for a drink	b) swimming	c) to a movie	d) some friends
3	You listen to	a) music	b) the teacher	c) the radio	d) shopping
4	You buy	a) a book	b) some shoes	c) a coffee	d) a friend
5	You have	a) long hair	b) a coffee	c) twenty years	d) breakfast

b Complete the sentences with a verb + noun combination from exercise 1a.

You can ....*read a newspaper*.......... if you want to read about the news.

1 I don't .... because I don't like sports.

2 Good students .... when she is talking.

3 After work we sometimes .... in a bar.

4 You can .... in a bookstore.

5 I always .... in a cafe, on the way to work.

2 Pronunciation

Write the past forms of these irregular verbs. Use the list of irregular verbs at the back of the Student's Book to help you if you want. Then match the past forms which have the same sound.

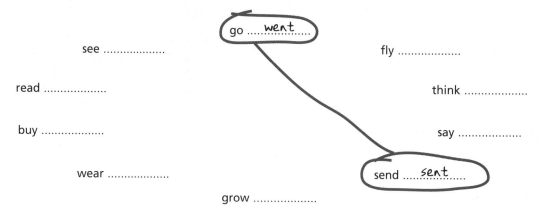

go .....*went*.....

see ....

read ....

buy ....

wear ....

grow ....

fly ....

think ....

say ....

send .....*sent*.....

3 Language work

Complete the description of Kate's journey. Use the verbs in the box in the past simple form.

buy wait fly see be go arrive have meet read

Kate (1) ....*waited*.... at the airport check-in. At last she (2) .... her husband, James.
They (3) .... lunch at the airport restaurant and Kate (4) .... a book from the airport
bookstore. They (5) .... to Cape Town – a long journey. On the plane they (6) .... their
books. They (7) .... tired when they (8) .... Kate's sister (9) .... them at the
airport and they (10) .... to her house by taxi.

4 Skills work: reading

a Rory Bruno is a radio DJ. He lives in London.
Read the article and write the names of the days on the map,
next to the correct place.

On Sunday I played at Exeter University. When I got home I listened to new CDs for about two and a half hours. On Monday I went to Warrington to broadcast the show. I was on air for four hours – it was great. I stayed there for the night and on Tuesday I went to Manchester for a meeting. On Wednesday I recorded a radio commercial back in London and went shopping for new CDs. On Thursday I lived real life – stayed at home and did some washing! On Friday I was DJ at a club in Newcastle. When I got home I lay on the sofa with a glass of red wine!

b Now mark these sentences T (true) or F (false).

Rory Bruno had a busy week.   T ✓ F ○

1 He worked every day.   T ○ F ○

2 He traveled a lot.   T ○ F ○

3 He stayed in Warrington for two nights. T ○ F ○

4 He worked on Friday.   T ○ F ○

> **Glossary**
> *DJ*: someone who plays CDs on the radio or in a club.
> *broadcast*: you broadcast a radio or television show.
> *on air*: when you are recording a show you are on air.

2 Famous lives

1 Word work: the arts

a Look at the words and names in the box. Do they refer to music or art? Complete the spidergram.

> Yehudi Menuhin   composer   Dali   musician   violin   auditorium
> painting   Picasso   artist   Mozart   gallery

music

Yehudi Menuhin

art

Dali

b Can you write more words on the spidergram?

c Complete the sentences with words from the spidergram in exercise 1a.

Yehudi Menuhin played and taught ...the violin... .

1 Mozart was an Austrian ....

2 The Tate .... is in London.
You can see many paintings there.

3 There are more than 100 ....
in the orchestra.

4 Picasso was a famous Catalan .... ,
who painted "Guernica".

5 We went to a concert at the new ....

Menuhin

Dali

Language summary: past simple (*yes / no* questions)

Form:
Past simple questions are formed with *did*. The form is the same for all persons.
The verb *be* is different – there is no auxiliary *did*.

Did	you she they	go to the gallery? like the painting? eat the food?	Yes, No,	you she they	did. didn't. (did not.)
Was	he	happy?	Yes, he was. No, he wasn't (was not).		
Were	they	at the disco?	Yes, they were. No, they weren't (were not).		

2 Language work

a Circle the correct answer.

Did you go out last night?

a) Yes, I was.   b) Yes, I didn't.   c) Yes, I did.

1 Were they at work yesterday?

a) Yes, they was.   b) No, they weren't.   c) No, you weren't.

2 Did Mr. Jones see the dentist?

a) Yes, he saw.   b) Yes, did he.   c) Yes, he did.

3 Was the lesson difficult?

a) No, it wasn't.   b) No, I wasn't.   c) No, it didn't.

4 Did they like the painting?

a) Yes, they liked.   b) Yes, it is.   c) No, they didn't.

5 Did you see John at the art gallery?

a) Yes, I did.   b) Yes, I was.   c) Yes, he did.

b Put the words in the correct order to form questions.

composer / Picasso / was / a?   _Was Picasso a composer?_

1 weekend / play / soccer / you / did / the / on? .... ?

2 you / born / this / were / town / in? .... ?

3 school / week / last / come / you / did / to? .... ?

4 parents / your / did / today / work? .... ?

5 "Sunflowers" / paint / Van Gogh / did? .... ?

6 artists / were / Dali / Picasso / and? .... ?

7 Spain / in / did / Van Gogh / live ? .... ?

c Answer the questions in exercise 2b. Use short answers.

No, he wasn't.

1 ....   4 ....

2 ....   5 ....

3 ....   6 ....

     7 ....

3 Pronunciation work

Circle the word that has a different vowel sound from the others in each group.

     a) flew   b) two   c) too   d) know

1 a) die   b) buy   c) say   d) fly

2 a) beef   b) she   c) bread   d) meet

3 a) love   b) come   c) lose   d) fun

4 a) bought   b) boat   c) taught   d) lost

5 a) came   b) rain   c) play   d) said

3 Epic journeys

> **Language note**
>
> You *discover* something that existed before you saw it.
>
> You *invent* something for the first time.

1 Word work: discoveries and inventions

a Match the famous person with an invention or discovery.

Who?	What?
1 Marie Curie	a) penicillin
2 Christopher Columbus	b) jeans
3 John Logie Baird	c) America
4 Alexander Graham Bell	d) radium
5 Levi Strauss	e) the television
6 Louis Pasteur	f) the telephone

b Now write a sentence about each famous person in exercise 1a. Use *invent* or *discover*.

1 Marie Curie discovered radium.

2 ....

3 ....

4 ....

5 ....

6 ....

c Which discovery or invention was the most important? Give a reason for your choice.

I think ....

....

2 Language work

Correct the sentences with a short answer. Then give the true answer if you can!

Christopher Columbus was French.   No he was'nt. He was Italian.

1 Marie Curie discovered helium.   ....

2 Van Gogh was American.   ....

3 Alexander Graham Bell discovered the telephone.   ....

4 John Logie Baird invented the computer.   ....

5 Picasso was a scientist.   ....

3 Word work: travel

a Find ten travel words in the word square.

B	A	L	L	O	O	N	J
I	R	S	A	I	L	E	O
W	R	F	R	A	D	V	U
P	I	L	O	T	R	O	R
S	V	I	U	M	I	Y	N
H	E	G	T	B	V	A	E
I	Y	H	G	Z	E	G	Y
P	F	T	R	A	V	E	L

b Complete the sentences with words from the word square in exercise 3a.

His train ....*journey*.... started in Paris and ended in Turkey.

1 We flew from London to Rome. The .... lasted two hours.

2 A .... flies a plane or balloon.

3 The cheapest way to .... is by bus.

4 Breitling Orbiter 3 is the name of a ....

5 I don't have a car because I can't ....

6 Columbus .... from Spain to America.

> **Language note**
> A *journey* is a noun.
> To *travel* is a verb,
> but can be an abstract noun:
> *It was a long journey.* (noun)
> *I traveled by train.* (verb)
> *Travel is fun.* (noun)

4 Skills work: writing

a Complete the text with the words in the box.

coffee	arrive	go	work	takes	about	bus	at	thirty	o'clock

I leave (1) ....*work*.... at seven (2) .... and arrive

(3) .... the language school at about half past seven.

It (4) .... me about (5) .... minutes. I travel

by (6) .... When I (7) .... I usually have some

(8) .... before the class. After the class I usually

(9) .... home. My trip home takes me

(10) .... forty-five minutes.

> **Language note**
> Notice how we use the verb *take*:
> *I leave at 6:00 and arrive at 7:00. It*
> *takes (me) one hour.*

b Now write in a similar way about your trip to the place where you study English.

I ....

....

Unit 12 Past and future goals

1 Life events

1 Word work: life events

a Look at the words in the box.
Are they associated with weddings, funerals or both?
Complete the word map.

church	bride	white dress
cemetery	black clothes	death
presents	flowers	happy
honeymoon	sad	

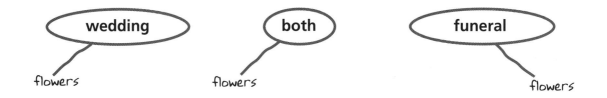

wedding

flowers

both

flowers

funeral

flowers

b Can you write more words on the word map?

2 Word work: collocations

a Match the verbs with the nouns / adjectives to make common collocations.

Verb	Noun/Adjective
1 You win	a) an exam / a test.
2 You pass	b) from high school / college.
3 You move	c) a race / a competition.
4 You get	d) to a new place.
5 You graduate	e) married / a new job.

b Which events in exercise 2a have you experienced? Write three sentences about your own experiences.

I won a tennis competition in 1998.

2 ....

1 ....

3 ....

3 Word work: expressions with *get*

Complete the sentences with the correct form of *get* and the words in the box.

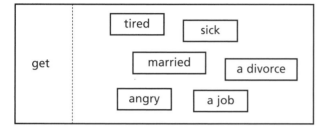

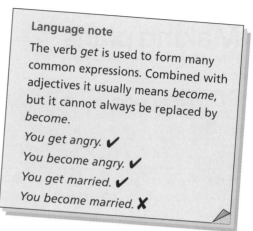

Language note

The verb *get* is used to form many common expressions. Combined with adjectives it usually means *become*, but it cannot always be replaced by *become*.

You get angry. ✔
You become angry. ✔
You get married. ✔
You become married. ✘

I .....*get tired*..... when I work late in the evenings.

1 My wife and I .... in 1975. We have been together for more than 25 years!

2 I graduated this summer and want to .... in an office.

3 My sister and her husband .... last year and now she lives alone.

4 When my sister spilled coffee on my new dress I ....

5 My brother .... when he traveled in India.

4 Skills work: reading

Read the article about Jude Peroni. Then circle the correct words to make the sentences true.

Jude traveled with her (sister) / brother.

1 *Her sister / A person they didn't know* died in Vietnam.

2 The people they met were *friendly / unfriendly*.

3 They went to a *funeral / wedding* at the temple.

4 It was a *sad / happy* occasion.

5 Jude has a *positive / negative* impression of Vietnam.

Glossary

nun: a religious woman who lives in a women's religious community

JUDE PERONI TALKS ABOUT HER TRIP TO ASIA

"I went to Vietnam with my sister in 1994. It was a fantastic trip. We arrived in the south, and spent three weeks traveling up to the north and then left from Ho Chi Minh City. Vietnam is very beautiful and special. The people are so lovely – we experienced real kindness there.

On one occasion we were in a small village and visited a temple. I suppose it was Buddhist. The funeral of one of the nuns was taking place and so they were having a party in her honor. They invited us to stay and we had a delicious vegetarian lunch with them. It was so different from a funeral in America, where people from outside are not welcome. It was a joyful, positive occasion. Amazing."

71

2 Making plans

Language summary: future with *going to*			
Use:			
Use *going to* for definite future plans.			
Form:			
I'm (am)	going to	cook dinner.	
		buy a new car.	
He isn't (is not)		travel around Europe.	
Is she	going to	take a course?	Yes, she is. / No, she isn't.
		get married?	
Are they		play basketball?	Yes, they are. / No they aren't.

1 Language work

a What are their plans? Put the words in the correct order to form sentences.

sell / Peter / bicycle / is / to / going / his   Peter is going to sell his bicycle.

1 August / Bill / take / going / a / in / is / to / vacation ....

2 wine / I'm / have / to / going / glass / a / of ....

3 tomorrow / parents / are / my / leave / going / to ....

4 golf / going / Frances / to / is / play ....

5 children / soccer / the / are / play / going / to ....

b Match the sentences with the people in the pictures. Then form questions about them using the words in parentheses.

..D.. June's going to college.

(what / she / study?) _What's she going to study?_

3 ...... Tim's going to get married.

(who / he / marry?) ....

1 ...... I'm going to a party tonight.

(what / you / wear?) ....

4 ...... Mom and Dad are going to visit friends.

(who / they / visit?) ....

2 ...... Jim's going to Thailand on vacation.

(where / he / stay?) ....

5 ...... Georgia's going to paint her room.

(what color / she / paint it?) ....

c **Make the sentences negative using the words in parentheses.**

She's going to wear blue.

(not black) _She isn't going to wear black._

1 They're going to play baseball.

(not volleyball) ....

2 I'm going to visit my mother.

(not my father) ....

3 You're going to work in Poland.

(not Austria) ....

4 He's going to leave at 6:00.

(not 7:00) ....

Language note

Remember the negative forms of the verb *be*.

She's not. / She isn't. ✔

We're not. / We aren't. ✔

I'm not. ✔

I amn't. ✗

2 **Word work:** activities

a **Match the verbs with the correct nouns.**
Then write one more noun to match each verb.

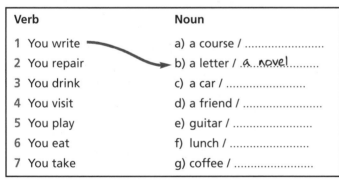

Verb	Noun
1 You write	a) a course / ....
2 You repair	b) a letter / .a. novel..........
3 You drink	c) a car / ....
4 You visit	d) a friend / ....
5 You play	e) guitar / ....
6 You eat	f) lunch / ....
7 You take	g) coffee / ....

I'm going to write a novel.

b **Write three plans for yourself using the verb and noun combinations in exercise 2a.**

1 I'm going to .... after this class.

2 .... on the weekend.

3 ....

3 Good advice

Language summary: *should / shouldn't*
Use:
Use *should* to express advice.
Form:
• For statements: subject + *should(n't)* + main verb.
• For questions: *should* + subject + main verb.
• The form is the same for all persons.

You	should	ask the teacher.			
She	shouldn't	smoke.			

Should	he they	tell her?	Yes, No,	he they	should. shouldn't.

1 Language work

a Match the problem with the appropriate advice.

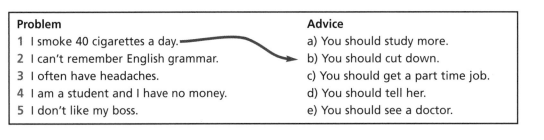

Problem	Advice
1 I smoke 40 cigarettes a day.	a) You should study more.
2 I can't remember English grammar.	b) You should cut down.
3 I often have headaches.	c) You should get a part time job.
4 I am a student and I have no money.	d) You should tell her.
5 I don't like my boss.	e) You should see a doctor.

b Complete the sentences with *should* or *shouldn't*.

You ...*should*... study before you take an exam.

1 Children .... eat too many sweets.

2 You .... drink and drive.

3 Vegetarians .... sometimes take a vitamin supplement.

4 Smokers .... ask before lighting a cigarette at the dinner table.

2 Skills work: reading

a Do you agree or disagree with the following statements? Check the boxes to show your opinion.

	Agree	Disagree
1 Children should play outside more.	○	○
2 Parents should have at least two children.	○	○
3 Spending time on computers can lead to to weight problems.	○	○
4 Fast food can lead to weight problems.	○	○

b Which arguments from exercise 2a are mentioned in the article? Check the boxes.

1 ◯   2 ◯   3 ◯   4 ◯

Where is it going to end?

Jimmy George is 13 years old, but he can't wear his school uniform. He's too big! Jimmy weighs 100 kg. His favorite meal is chicken and french fries. That's one whole chicken and a big plate of fried potatoes. He also loves chocolate, cola and cookies.

Expert dietician Jenny Murray says "This is a very worrying trend. Children like Jimmy should be educated to eat well and maintain a normal weight. If not, they will grow up to be obese, with health problems."

It appears that children are experiencing more and more health problems because of their sedentary lifestyles and the wrong sort of diet. Children are spending more and more time at school using computers instead of playing sports and enjoying other outdoor activities.

Glossary
fast food: convenience food like hamburgers and french fries, which are usually high in fats and sugar
obese: a medical word for *overweight*
sedentary: not moving. A desk job is a *sedentary* job.

c What advice would you give Jimmy? Use *should* and *shouldn't*.

You should cut down on chocolate.

....

....

3 Pronunciation work

Put the words in the correct column, according to the stress.

| ceremony | experience | technology | information | discovery | secondary | dictionary |
| graduation | activity | professional | relationship | sedentary |

Oooo	oOoo	ooOo
ceremony	experience	information

A Learner training

1 Grammar terms

The Workbook and the Student's Book use some English grammar words. It is important to know these basic terms: *noun, singular, plural, verb, adverb, adjective,* and *contraction.*

Task 1
Study the table and examples. Add your own examples or put a translation in the last column.

Grammar word	Meaning	Example	Your example or translation
noun	thing or person	*book, doctor*	
singular	one thing or person	*table, student*	
plural	two or more things or people	*tables, students.*	
verb	activity	*I **work** in a bank.*	
adverb	describes a verb	*You sing **beautifully**.*	
adjective	describes a thing or person	*a **tall** person.*	
contraction	short form	*She's Chinese.*	

Task 2
Put the words in the correct column in the table.

> he's blue teachers come aggressively do actor excellent hotel cars slowly I'm

Singular noun	Plural noun	Verb	Adverb	Adjective	Contraction
					he's

Language note
Some words can be the same for more than one grammar form:
a discount (n)
to discount (v)
For this reason, it is always a good idea to note the part of speech in your vocabulary notebook.

2 Recording vocabulary

It is important to record basic information about new vocabulary. It's also a good idea to use abbreviations for different types of word: *noun (n)*

Task 3

Write abbreviations for these types of word:

Verb   (................)   Adverb   (................)   Adjective   (................)

It is also important to record:

• word stress   • part of speech (use abbreviations)   • difficult sounds for you   • an example

literature (n)
I love reading and I studied literature in university.
This will help you to remember and to use the words correctly later.

It can be easier to remember vocabulary if you organize it into groups and give examples. Here are some ways to organize vocabulary found in this book.

1 By theme:
   Jobs
   I'm a sales representative.
   I work in a company.

2 By word class:
   Verb: to work
   Noun: a worker
   You work hard [adv].

3 Alphabetically:
   A
   alphabet
   Australia

4 In a spidergram:

tennis — relaxation activities — swimming
listening to music — relaxation activities — watching TV

Task 4
Choose an area of vocabulary. Decide on the best technique to record it.

B Spelling rules

Rule 1: Contractions

Contractions (contracted verb forms) are used in the Workbook and the Student's Book.
Use apostrophes to show where letters are missing in contracted forms:
*I **don't** (do not) speak Russian.*
In English, contractions are common when people speak, and when they write to friends, for example.
Using contractions sounds natural. Recognizing them also makes listening easier.
I am = I'm   I am not = I'm not

Task 1

Write the contracted forms

She is Italian. <u>She's Italian.</u>

1 I am from Spain. ....

2 I cannot swim. ....

3 He does not like dancing. ....

4 Where is the art museum? ....

5 We are going on vacation in June. ....

Rule 2: Apostrophes to indicate possession

Apostrophes are also used to indicate possession.
*John**'s** book = the book that belongs to John.*

Rule 3: Capital letters

Use capital letters for:
• names of places and people: *Jane lives in London.*
• names of days, months: *They came here on Wednesday.*
• languages and nationality: *She's French and she speaks French.*
• the beginning of a sentence: *Her mother **is** very angry.*

> **Language note**
> Use question marks only at the end of a question:
> *What's your name?*

Task 2

Rewrite the text by using capital letters where necessary.

M
~~m~~y name is john. i'm an english teacher. i live in caracas. i came to live here in july. i speak russian and spanish very well.

Rule 4: Plurals

- To form plural nouns, we usually add *"-s"*:
  a car – two cars
- When nouns end in *"-y"* after a consonant, change the *"-y"* to *"-ie"* and add *"-s"*:
  a baby – two babies
- When nouns end in *"-ch"* or *"-sh"*, add *"-es"*:
  a church – two churches
- There are some irregular plurals:
  man – men, child – children, person – people

Language note
Uncountable nouns do not take a plural form.
Cheese is nice ✔
Cheeses are nices ✗

Language note
Adjectives do not take a plural form.
a **nice** boy ✔
two **nice** boys ✔
two nices boys ✗

Task 3
Rewrite the text using the plural where necessary.

Rome is the capital of Italy. There are many person in Rome. The church/*es* are very famous. The food is delicious there. The weather is very good too. In summer we like to go to one of the park.

Macmillan Education
Between Towns Road, Oxford OX4 3PP
A division of Macmillan Publishers Limited
Companies and representatives throughout the world

ISBN 978 0 333 92655 0

Text © Macmillan Publishers Limited 2001

Design and illustration © Macmillan Publishers Limited 2001

First published 2001

Designed by Oliver Hickey.

Illustrated by Martin Aston, Andy Warrington and Geoff Waterhouse.

Cover photograph by Stone

The authors and publishers would like to thank the following for permission
to reproduce their photographs:
Mitchell Gerber/ Corbis p48(c), Bradley Smith/ Corbis p66(r); Ronald
Grant Cinema Archive p48 (fl,fr); Rex Features pp48 (l,r), 66(l); Stone
pp14, 17, 21, 23, 33, 68, 71

Printed and bound in Thailand

2012 2011 2010 2009 2008
15   14   13   12   11